You Rock!

Stop

Looking for a
Husband

Stop

Looking for a
Husband

{ Find the Love of Your Life }

MARINA SBROCHI

Brown Books Publishing Group
Dallas, Texas

Stop Looking for a Husband
Find the Love of Your Life

Brown Books Publishing Group
16200 North Dallas Parkway, Suite 170
Dallas, Texas 75248
www.brownbooks.com
(972) 381-0009

A New Era in Publishing.™

ISBN 978-1-934812-90-7
Library of Congress Control Number 2010938737

Printing in the United States.
10 9 8 7 6 5 4 3 2 1

For more information about the book or the author, please visit www.StopLookingForAHusband.com.

Acknowledgments

I would like to thank my mother, Mary Jo, for always encouraging me to do something that makes me happy. Thanks also to the many friends who contributed their stories of the good, the bad, and the ugly; to all the random people I polled with many, many questions; to my editor, Alison Miller, my publisher, Milli Brown, and the staff at Brown Books; to Webb—I wasn't even looking and there you were.

Contents

Author's Note

I grew up believing in the *Cinderella* fairy tale—you know, go to college, meet the man of your dreams, get married, have the kids, the house, the cars—and as I grew older, my quest for Prince Charming was never far from the back of my mind.

People say the only way to really learn is to make a mistake, and I have to agree. As I dated . . . and dated . . . and dated my way through my twenties, I realized a few things. First and foremost, I couldn't find happiness in another person. What? That's right—I couldn't find happiness in another person. Sound selfish? Maybe, at first glance. But trust me—figuring that out changed my life forever.

Once upon a time I thought, *If only I had this great guy, life would be perfect! If he was good-looking and successful, and seemed like he'd make a great father, what more could I want? A missing glass slipper?* At age thirty, I married the guy who was perfect on paper. Two children and six years later, I realized that on-paper perfection did not a marriage make.

After that pivotal *aha!* moment, I put the focus on myself. Strangely enough, wonderful things began to happen. I learned lots about who I am and even more about what a solid, lasting relationship is made of. Sometimes you can only find what you want by experiencing what you don't want. Luckily for you, I've made many mistakes along the way—as have my friends—and I'm here to share them with you.

Just call me the smart-ass been-there-done-that version of Dear Abby. Everyone has that friend they call when they need relationship advice, and I've been in steady business since college, when I counseled my six female roommates through an endless string of relationships and one-night stands. I was eternally at the ready to hear their accounts of glory and failure. I have seen attraction between two people that was as strong as gravity. Other times there was a repulsion so fierce it was like accidentally walking in on your grandparents doing the deed. Yet when things actually worked out, it all seemed so effortless—so serendipitous.

The most vital lesson I've learned is that true love magically appears when you're being yourself, doing things for yourself, and creating opportunities to share that with others. What follows is a series of true dating tales—some awkward, some blissful, and some downright dirty. They all provide insight into the frustrating emotional adventure that is dating. In a world where advice is constantly hammered into our heads from every angle, it's nice to just sit back and think that it really can be so *serendipitous.*

1

You Rock

Fed up with the rules and how-tos of landing your dream guy? *Seven Foolproof Ways to Meet Your Mate? How to Land the Man of Your Dreams?* If it sounds like a crock, that's because it is. The truth is, there is no foolproof method. Why? Because—surprise!—everyone is different. Some people think of an ideal first date as dinner and a movie. Others would rather go skydiving.

So what is one to do in this confusing world of strangers and fix-ups where no two are alike? Breathe easy, girls, because the single most important thing you can do is also the most effortless: be yourself. It's the only way you'll find your perfect mate.

Here's the sad-but-true tale of someone who chose to disregard this ever-important rule. Don't let it happen to you.

The Seafaring Storyteller

A friend of mine meets a guy with an unstoppable passion for sailing. She goes absolutely gaga for him—and they're off to a great start. When he asks if she shares his love for wind and water, she replies with a very enthusiastic, "Yes! I love sailing!" Two weeks later, they're in Miami for a jaunt on his 30-foot Catalina. Just as they push off from the dock, the terror sets in.

My friend is deathly afraid of water. Of course, she's never been sailing. She's freaking out! Sailor Jerry turns the boat around and buys her a seat on the next flight home, figuring that if she can't tell him the truth about something as basic as a hobby, they certainly can't have a meaningful relationship.

Had the aforementioned girlfriend consulted me, I would have advised her to say, "I want to be honest with you. Water scares me, but it's only because I had a bad experience as a child. But if you help me, I'd love to try to get over my fear." The sailor would have gently eased her through her fears and they would be tooling around the Caribbean sipping piña coladas right now.

Stop the Chaos

How do you stop this pattern? First, you have to stop lying to yourself.

You convince yourself that you love camping, when in reality your definition of "roughing it" is staying at the Holiday Inn instead of the Ritz.

You gladly tell the hot new guy from Spain that you speak Spanish. Truth be told, the only Spanish you know is, "Si, Ortega!"

"I love the country!" says the city mouse who gets asthma from just looking at horses.

We lie because we want people to like us. Why would a guy like you if you don't share the same interests, right? Wrong! Don't be embarrassed by what you like—embrace it! Be yourself! Besides, one of the biggest thrills of dating is introducing your mate to your favorite places, foods, and life pursuits. You cannot build a meaningful relationship on a lie.

Another tip on being yourself: You know you the best. You'll never have to come up with a story about what you like and what you don't like. You won't have to look up your morals and beliefs because you know them. Besides, like my mother always said, it's much easier to remember the truth than it is to remember a lie.

Don't Febreze™ Dirty Laundry

Prior to even thinking about your physical appearance, you have to take an honest look at what you're wearing inside. We all have little quirks, past relationships, and everyday problems. Those are part of life. If you're not in a mentally stable place, however, then stop right now. You must take care of unresolved issues before you involve anyone else. Talk to a therapist or a trusted friend, and whittle your emotional baggage down to one carry-on item.

Love Thyself. And Count The Ways.

Take some time to think about all your positive at-tributes (if this takes all day, good for you!). Write them down and don't be shy. Sometimes we truly forget how wonderful we are, and we need a written list to remind ourselves. I like to tape this list to my bathroom mirror, but you can put it anywhere. Carry it in your pocket or in your purse, and reread it as much as necessary. When I say "positive attributes," I mean both physical and nonphysi-cal. You're awesome and you know it, so don't skimp. Do you love yourself? Really, do you? You have to. Because if you don't, no one else will.

Pick Me! Pick Me!

Too often we find ourselves haunted by the pressure of dating, like self-conscious middle-schoolers anxious that nobody will pick us to play on the team. We run around like crazed teenagers, trying too hard to make ourselves desirable, trying to be someone we're not. Listen closely: this never works. Treat this advice like the gospel: the most important thing you can do is be yourself.

Confidence: The Secret Aphrodisiac

I know a beautiful girl with a wonderful career and a great figure. She's smart. She's sassy. She's a hell of a good dancer. Unfortunately she has the confidence of a four-hundred-pound person with Coke-bottle glasses and acne.

She constantly tells me, "I'm not pretty," "I don't look good in this," "I'm not funny," "I can't talk in a group."

Jeez Louise! Slit my wrists, why don't you? After saying "Oh, yes you are" about a hundred times, I'm worn out! Not to mention that my reassurance is wasted: even after I tell her how wonderful she is, she still shoots herself down.

If you think a guy wants to battle your negativity all the time, you are thoroughly disillusioned. No one wants to skip around a black hole. Besides, if you keep telling him what a sorry person you are, he might just believe you— and skedaddle. Hello, friend—if you're still in there— come out! It's positively nice out here if you believe me and believe in yourself!

On another note, one of the most attractive guys I know is not someone who would cause most girls to spin around for a double-take. But once he opens his mouth, you can't help falling in love. What is this mysterious, fun, and comforting quality he exudes? Confidence. This guy is smart and cool and fun, and he knows it. He is genuinely interested in others. He engages people in conversation. Confidence radiates from his every word and movement.

You have to believe in yourself, you have to respect yourself, and you have to be sure of yourself. By doing this, first and foremost, you're doing yourself a favor. You're the biggest fan of you! So don't shortchange yourself. You're number one—believe it and know it. There is nothing more unattractive than a woman who doesn't believe in herself.

I Said Confidence, Not Cockiness

Please don't confuse the two. There is a huge difference between them, and if you cross the invisible line, there is no hope for your love life. Confidence is the state of thinking positively of oneself and one's actions. Cockiness is overconfidence cloaked in rudeness—it's almost as unattractive as having zero confidence. You know cocky when you see it and hear it. It's surefire man-repellent. So don't be cocky. It will alienate you and get you uninvited to parties as quickly as the piggy flu.

2

Desperation Stinks

When you're on the hunt for a man, everyone can smell it. It's like you're wearing a fragrance that I like to call *Desperado*. Believe me, ladies, it doesn't smell good. It reeks for miles! Not to mention it's guaranteed man-repellent.

Blogging for a Husband

On February 16, 2010, a Dallas woman named Lisa Linehan created a blog called Project Husband. Two days later, she booked a venue for her wedding—a 14,000-square-foot stone-façade spread with massive crystal chandeliers and a groom's suite equipped with an Xbox 360 (lucky guy). You can find this over-the-top event space on an episode of the television show *Platinum*

Weddings. Seriously—she's already planned her wedding, right down to the DJ and photographer. There's only one thing missing—a groom. I kid you not.

Here is how I imagine her first date with a prospective Mr. Linehan. Let me set the scene: it's August 2010, in a coffee shop.

Lisa: Hey there, so . . . what are you doing on February 15 of 2011?

Dude: Um, I'm sorry, what was your name again?

Lisa: It's Lisa. Do you by chance like Colleyville, Texas? How do you feel about an '80s cover band?

Dude: What's in Colleyville? '80s cover bands . . . you mean, like you want to go see one?

Lisa: No, silly! I'm just trying to see if you are available to marry me next year. Everything's booked! All you have to do is show up!

Seriously? Seriously?! What kind of guy would agree to something like this? Talk about putting the cart before the horse. The horse might not even show up! I would agree with most men when they say that women are always trying to rush through the phases of a relationship. They say they feel pressure to get married. Here, my friends, is exhibit A. Is it any wonder the divorce rate is so high? Women are marrying for the wrong reasons. Picking a guy simply to fill a spot in your wedding album is not a good idea.

Stop Yammering

Also known as "relax and chill." You need to practice this rule in a variety of ways. Let's start with talking. This is for all you gum-flappers and nervous chatterers. You don't have to tell each new person you meet your entire life story—especially on the first date. Save something to talk about on your next twenty dates (and the next twenty years).

Solid relationships take time to form. Your best friend didn't become your best friend overnight. You slowly got to know each other and gradually shared information. The same rule applies in dating. Your potential future boyfriend, no matter how interested he is in you, does not want to listen to you recount every single one of your childhood memories in the first twenty minutes of the date. Nor does he need you to confess to every incident where you've shown less than perfect judgment. Talk about putting your worst foot forward!

Leave Some Skeletons in the Closet

I'm not telling you to hide all of your skeletons, but you should definitely keep some of them in the closet until it's appropriate to share. This depends on how scary that skeleton is. Did you have a nose job? That can come pretty early in the game, but it probably doesn't matter if you disclose that in the first month or the fifth month. Divorced? Kids? These should be disclosed on date number one. Your children should be most important to you, and you should know whether that's a deal-breaker for your potential mate. Did you shoplift at sixteen? Sure, that's sketchy, but did you learn a lesson and never do it again? Are you so scarred that you haven't even borrowed clothes since? You can bring that out when you've formed some rapport. We've all done things we're not proud of. These moments don't define you—they just make you a more interesting person.

Politics and Religion

Likewise, we all have opinions. People love getting worked up about politics and religion. If it's super important to you that someone share your exact beliefs, then by all means, bring it up. Gently. If you can accept that people can agree to disagree, you may want to slowly express your opinion on certain topics as they arise. You'll find that once people get to know each other, they're more accepting. You should never change your opinions solely to make a relationship work.

Show Some Restraint. Please

Starting to like the guy? Even though you may be picking out wedding gowns and flowers in your head, temper those thoughts until you've been proposed to. There's nothing wrong with expressing your feelings, and you should not be scared to tell someone how much you like him. But we all know that when things are going well, the tendency to get excited—really, really excited—is sometimes unavoidable. Go ahead: Jump up and down. Do cartwheels. Sing Madonna songs at the top of your lungs. Do it in the privacy of your own home though, unless you want to scare away Prince Charming.

I'm of the mind-set that one should play a little defense here. Just because your first three dates are perfect does not mean it's time to declare your undying love. Feel free to call your best friend and tell her that you've found the person with whom you're going to spend the rest of your life, but please resist the urge to tell *him* at this juncture in your dating career. Tell him you enjoy his company. Tell him what a wonderful time you had last night. Do not ask him what color he thinks you should paint the walls when you move in together or if he always thought he'd get married in a church or on the beach.

Breathing Room

I know that many people advocate playing hard to get. In theory, it works. You act like you don't have time for him; he finds you exponentially more attractive. It's the thrill of the chase. Problem is, this little game can quickly spin out of control. You both get so busy playing hard to get that you may never actually hang out. Or you start creating lies about why you're so busy all the time, and pretty soon you're trying to navigate your own tangled web of untruths.

I prefer to go the route of creating some space. Even if you think you really want to, don't spend every second with someone from the moment you meet him. The worst thing that can happen when you fall for a guy is to lose your identity. Just ask all your friends—if you still have any.

We all know someone (guy or girl) who falls off the face of the earth when they're dating someone. This is destructive behavior, and I'll tell you why. The goal is not to assume someone else's life. The goal is to find a partner and share a life that has two equal parts. I realize that sometimes after we've paired up and have families, we spend less time with friends than we did in our single years. This is the natural progression of growing up. Still, this does not mean that you toss out years of friendship for someone or give up the things you care about. Ever.

In the same vein, if your new beau is always knocking on your door, don't you begin to wonder if he has his own life? Interests? Hobbies? Friends? Just as you are not to lose yourself, you don't want to let him latch onto your life. You have your own life; he has his. Together you will have something new.

3

Looks Matter

t's another girls' night out. Four friends have it on their minds to drink, dance, and find someone for Mindy to hang out with. Mind you, we are not husband-shopping for her—just trying to find her a guy she can make out with and possibly, at a later occasion, eat food or see a movie with.

The plan is to meet at my house at eight for a glass of wine and some discussion of our destination, then take off. *Ding-dong.* I open the door, and to my great horror I see Mindy dressed in mom jeans that conjure up none other than Ed Grimley. (If you're unfamiliar with this *Saturday Night Live* character, picture this: Martin Short with his pants pulled up to his chest, hair gelled into a cone at the front of his head, and a walk that reminds me of a controlled seizure.)

Her jeans are up past her navel. She's wearing a green turtleneck sweater from the '80s. And glasses. Too-bright pink lipstick, extreme blush, and hair that hasn't been brushed since this morning add to the unnerving effect.

Me: Hey. Mindy! So . . . did you want to get ready over here?

Mindy: No, why? I'm ready to go.

Me: Where? An '80s party?

Mindy: No, out! Tonight!

Me: Mindy, we need to talk.

Mindy: No, go out.

Me: We need to talk. Seriously.

Mindy: Is it the glasses?

Me: Yes. And the clothes, and the makeup, and the hair. Mindy, you're a pretty girl with a great personality. Don't hide it under this ghastly getup. I'm not opposed to glasses, but the plastic frames you're wearing look like they're from the fifth grade. I know you have contacts, and I can see your eyes much better in them. Secondly, those jeans would be unflattering on Heidi Klum. I don't know who let you buy them, but they should be shot. You can borrow a pair of mine. Turtlenecks say, "I like the library and I don't like action." We aren't trying to send that message. I have a top that screams cool, fun party girl. You need to put it on ASAP before I start thinking of you as a schoolmarm. And I'm sorry to say, but I'm going to start fresh on your hair and makeup too.

Forty-five minutes and a bottle of wine later, Mindy's look had been transformed from *Eek!* to *Oh, yeah!* and I'm happy to report that she felt better about herself because of it. In the words of Fernando, another of my favorite *SNL* characters, "It is better to look good than to feel good!" Although truth be told, Mindy felt very good that night.

Everyone Knows It—But No One Admits It

Brace yourself, sit down, or pour yourself a tipple of whiskey, because I'm about to tell you something that everyone, from your elementary school teacher to your best friend, has been scared to say: looks matter.

What do you think draws a first glance when a person walks into a room? Sorry, it's not your beaming personality and your inner beauty (although it should be!). It's your body, what you're wearing, your facial appearance, and most importantly, your smile.

I'm not saying you have to look like Gisele Bündchen to get a man. What I'm saying is that you have to look the best you can possibly look. My first piece of advice may sound corny, and it might be something you've heard all your life, but I swear it's true: the absolute best thing you can wear is a smile.

Everyone looks great smiling, and everyone is attracted to a smile. It's comforting, it's approachable, and you can trust it. Just the act of smiling will put you in a better mood (and instantly put others in one too). So don't sell yourself short on the single easiest, free thing you can do to make yourself look great! It is undeniably the most stunning thing you can wear.

Hairdos (And Don'ts)

Go to the mirror and take a look. Do you see a hairstyle that screams, "I look ten years older than I should"? Do you have the same haircut you had in middle school? Is your hair platinum blonde with black roots? Are you seeing gray? Well then, it's time for an update.

Pick up one of the sixty-four magazines piled up next to your bed and start browsing. When you see a look you like, tear it out. Steer yourself toward facial features on the page that are similar to yours, and keep in mind that you don't want to spend half your life in the bathroom trying to recreate a freshly blown-out look that you'll never achieve. You want to be the best you, not the fake you that only looks good if someone else is doing your hair.

Let's talk length. If the length of your hair even remotely approaches Crystal Gayle's, stop reading and go immediately to your nearest salon, because ass-length (and beyond) hair has never looked good. For the love of God, find a cut and style that is appropriate for your features—and for this decade. Ask your stylist to recommend something, and don't be afraid to break your straight-down, parted-in-the-middle look, even if it's been twenty years in the making.

Let's talk color. Now I know just as well as you that there are a handful of women in this world who look absolutely stunning in gray (Helen Mirren, Emmylou Harris, and Meryl Streep among them). They're all over the age of fifty. So my advice to you—if you truly think you look stunning in gray—is to keep it. On the other hand, if you're younger than fifty and simply hanging onto some ridiculous *I've never dyed my hair and I sure as shit ain't gonna start now* ideal, get over it. Your looks will thank you, and guys will begin to ask you out instead of asking you if you need help crossing the street.

Check your blonde. Is it tuba-brass yellow? Do you look washed-out? Are your roots twelve shades darker than your color? If so, get it fixed.

Do you like some funk in your color? Red, green, or blue? Rock on! Cheers to you for not being afraid to be different. For all those people who say neon streaks send guys running the other direction—well, they may be right. But a guy like that wouldn't be a match for you anyway.

Put on Some Clothes, for Crying Out Loud

Bottom line: if you look like a slut, people will treat you like one. Skintight micro minis and bra tops are not for nonworking girls, if you know what I mean. Remember that saying "Leave something to the imagination"? You don't have to leave *everything* to the imagination, but please have some respect for yourself.

Forget about money for a second. You can find nice, flattering clothes without breaking the bank. You just have to know what to look for. Take an honest look at your figure and note its positive aspects. Do you have toned arms? Nice legs? Find clothes that accentuate the positive.

Shop your closet. If something doesn't look good on you or it's three sizes too small, bag it up and donate it. Don't forget to take an honest inventory of your shoes. Yes, people do look down.

Get the Junk Out of Your Trunk

Are you healthy? In shape? Do you work out? (Or do you consider a workout walking to the donut shop?) If there's junk in your trunk—and in your pantry—get rid of it.

Women come in all shapes and sizes, and yes, men like women in all shapes and sizes. The key here is to be as fit and healthy as you can be for your shape, size, and genetic makeup.

Not everyone has the metabolism of a hummingbird and not all of us are blessed with what magazines consider to be beautiful bodies. I strongly suggest you take an honest look at yourself naked. Instead of being the usual critic, take a look with fresh eyes. Find three things you love about your body and be proud of them!

Now find three things you don't love. Instead of beating yourself up, devise a plan for change. Start slowly and do it for you. Changing your body takes time, and doing it just so that someone else will like you will never work. Did you hear that? Changing yourself for someone else will never work. Don't forget that. You have to make healthy changes for yourself.

Got something that you can't change? Stop dwelling on it! We're programmed into thinking that only an unblemished body is a good body. I'm here to tell you that this is simply untrue. I've asked countless men, and while there are definitely a few meatheads that demand a sun-kissed, perfectly toned bod, I can assure you that anyone worth dating will not hold you to ridiculous standards. Besides, confidence outshines any imperfection.

I am a huge proponent of being healthy and in shape for many reasons, and looks are not the first of them. Looking better is the best side effect of being healthy. What kind of message does someone who doesn't take care of her body send to a potential mate? That she doesn't care for herself and can't get her life in order. Taking care of yourself is the number one thing you can do before you can attract anyone else.

Start with exercise. Take advantage of gym promotions that offer a free visit or meeting with a personal trainer. There are tons of yoga studios, bike paths, hiking trails, tennis courts, and golf courses. Find something you like to do, and get off your butt. Bonus motivation: you could just meet someone fabulous while doing any one of these activities.

But That's Not All

Now that you've got your sexy appearance nailed down, I'm going to throw a monkey wrench in the works. Looking great is hugely important to being your best and getting a date—but it's just the packaging. Say you have all the best ski gear money can buy: the fabulous jacket, the sleek goggles, great skinny ski pants, and top-notch skis. You may look dynamite, but if you can't get down that mountain, you're not fooling anyone.

For instance, you may have a great-looking girlfriend (there's one in every crowd, right?). You know the drill— heads turn when she walks through the door, people stop and help her with anything, she has to decline the lineup of free drinks sent her way. Go ahead and gag.

She's perfect until she opens her mouth. Maybe she's rude, maybe she's stuck-up, or maybe she's just clueless. So while she may get in the door, she isn't going to get much farther. Over time, this attractive woman will turn ugly because of her actions. So while looks do matter, I don't want you to get all wrapped up in physical appearance. Remember that it's just the wrapping paper. Be confident, happy, friendly, and kind—and work on showing off that smile.

You know why people like Derek Jeter? Because he's good-looking *and* he can hit a home run. Be the entire package.

4

Keep Your Cool

re you looking for a mate who has similar interests? Someone you're extremely attracted to? A person with whom you can hold a great conversation? Someone you can't live without? Or are you looking for a man who folds towels the same way you do? Went to a prestigious university? Played high school football? Perhaps a big boy that can throw his dirty clothes in the hamper? Someone who doesn't leave the seat up?

If you're hung up on some ridiculous list of acceptable traits that your dreamboat must possess, stop reading this book right now because I cannot help you. You have to get yourself out of the water that I call *shallow* and look for what really matters. Dating is about the big picture. If you fixate on all the little details, you will fail. (Not to mention, you'll be incredibly annoying as you spiral down to utter defeat.) So get over it! You'll never truly know a person unless you let go of your pet peeves and set your gaze beyond the superficial bullshit that won't matter at all when you're both sitting on the porch together fifty years from now. You could be rejecting your perfect match, all because you "only date guys with dark hair" or because "his car is always a mess."

The One Who Didn't Get Away

Ericka, a former college roommate and lifelong friend of mine, was eleven months into her illustrious dating career on eharmony.com. There had been legions of unsuccessful encounters—from Comic Book Boy, a navel-gazing dork who was writing a book about vampires because he sometimes wondered if he was one, to Bass Player Guy, who admitted to a recently ended relationship with a nineteen-year-old groupie who accused him of giving her an STD. There was even Pinochle Boy, the thirty-three-year-old aerospace engineer whose sole hobby was playing the card game every Wednesday night with a group of men nearly three times his age.

Just as Ericka was nearing the end of her rope—and the end of her subscription—she received a message from the man who will from here on out be referred to as Bald Guy. Thirty-year-old Ericka's red-flag radar included baldness (along with superhero obsessions and STDs), but the rest of his profile—interests in travel, food, and the Rolling Stones—looked promising. Besides, how could it get any worse than the guy who showed up to a date with a ten-dollar bill and the excuse that he'd lost his wallet? Admittedly, Ericka wasn't wowed by Bald Guy's profile photo—mainly because of the shiny bald head that was blinding her from seeing his shiny, perfect smile.

Things moved quickly after she responded to his message. Their "29 Dimensions of Compatibility" were spot-on, and they breezed through the Guided Communication phases of eHarmony matchmaking (the answering of a few noninvasive questions and the listing of each other's "Must Haves" and "Can't Stands"). In less than an hour, they were instant-messaging in real time.

Bald Guy: It's so refreshing to talk to someone whose first question isn't about the car I drive or how much I make. So where do you live in Columbus?

Ericka: Damn! I was just going to ask what you do. But only out of curiosity. I'm not a gold digger, I promise. I do just fine for myself, thank you very much! Oh, and I live downtown, near the university.

Bald Guy: Well, in that case, I'm an investment banker. I live in Malibu. In a castle with a moat. And a Ferrari.

Ericka: Alas, the eHarmony stars have aligned. I have found my prince.

Bald Guy: No, seriously—and a lot of girls think this is lame—I'm finishing up my second master's at Eastern Kentucky, but I live in Marion, so I make the four-hour drive every Monday and Friday.

Ericka: Doesn't sound like you have much time for dating. . . .

So he's bald, he's racking up student loans, and he's never around. Just as Ericka was counting the strikes against him, Bald Guy asked if he could give her a call on his drive back from school. *Oh, why not? Sure, okay. I'll give it a try,* she thought. That Friday, just as he said he would, he called. The voice on the other end was eerily familiar. Bald Guy sounded exactly like a good friend of hers from high school. In a strange way, it was comforting. And the conversation was captivating!

There was no lack of silence as BG and Ericka compared experiences on traveling in Costa Rica, a country they'd both visited the previous year. The commonalities continued. They had both gone to Ohio State as undergrads, enjoyed the same restaurants, biked the same trails—you get the idea. Several more enchanting phone conversations ensued. Ericka was beginning to get that flutter-in-the-tummy *I like him!* feeling. Sweet text messages entered their realm of communication. It was almost as if every time she thought about him she'd get a message or a call. (Her words, not mine.)

Finally he asked her out. She had the idea of meeting at her favorite sushi spot but wanted to hear his suggestion first. (As you know, where a guy wants to take you is a solid clue to his personality—and intentions.) Surprise! He picked the same place.

The phone calls had become so comfortable at this point that she didn't think she'd be nervous when they met, but of course, she was. He had a good handshake and a little bit of a Kentucky accent. Great smile. And . . . he was bald. After all the phone conversations, she'd mostly forgotten this oh-so-evident undesirable trait.

But here they were. As Ericka fought her uneasiness, the hostess sat them right next to two friends she hadn't seen in a year. How embarrassing to be on a blind date—with a bald guy—in front of your old friends. After the requisite "Hi! How are you doing?" in passing, Ericka and BG settled into their table. As soon as the conversation kicked in, she became less and less nervous.

Pretty soon dinner was done—but they weren't. They moved to the bar next door and talked into the wee hours. At the end of the night, he walked her to her car, and as she stood there thanking him—the driver's-side door like an iron curtain between them—he quickly, and awkwardly, swooped in for the kiss. The hurried, forced maneuver caught her totally off guard, and she began to stutter something in the way of "Easy, buddy!" but he was already at it again—this time grasping the side of her face and pulling her in. Things wrapped up quickly though, and she managed to stammer out a quick "OK, goodnight!" and slam the door shut before there was any awkward rehashing of the moment.

In the phone dates that followed, they both strategically dodged the subject of that evening's awkward event, and everything was moving along smoothly as usual. BG was to be out of town the following weekend, so Ericka agreed to a blind date set up by a friend. The blind date bore all the qualities that she'd normally go gaga for, but strangely enough, she found herself comparing his every move to Bald Guy's. Then, out of nowhere, a former eHarmony encounter, Ford Boy, started e-mailing again, which led to a phone call, which led to a date. But all she could think about was her phone call that night with BG.

Pretty soon he was back from his trip and anxious to get together. After dinner, they returned to the same bar where they'd stayed so long after their first date. He was sweet and confident and funny. She liked him. She *really* liked him.

Bald Guy ended up being the only one she wanted to see, and now she gets to see him every day. He's smart, he's funny, he's loyal, and she can be herself around him. They started dating in October and by January they were talking about living together. One night at that same sushi joint, Ericka's fortune mysteriously read *You will move to a wonderful new home within the year.* Four months later, she sold her house and bought a new one—with Bald Guy. During those whirlwind couple of months, another fortune said *Everything will now come your way.* Suffice to say, it did just that.

Cool School

Listen up, because the lesson here is vital. Ericka would still be lurking in the shadows of eharmony.com, wasting perfectly good evenings on creepsters and cocky, well-dressed womanizers if she had let BG's bald head—or that awkward first kiss—scare her away. The mantra is simple: Be Cool. Yep. Be Cool. I'm not talking about two-thumbs-up Fonz-style cool. I'm talking about not shutting down when you see something you think would never work for you. Trust me, being cool is not as easy as it sounds.

Let's define "cool." A cool person is someone who has the ability to relax and go with the flow. Cool is someone who is flexible, who still has a blast when there's a change of plans. Cool is someone who knows current events and can talk about them without dominating the conversation or shoving their opinion down anyone's throat. Cool is happy and willing to try new things. Cool is being friendly with all people and not believing you're better than anyone else. Cool knows when to be serious and when to be funny. Cool should define you. You'll find that most things run more smoothly when you put your cool on.

I can't stress enough that almost every guy I talk to wants a woman who can keep her cool. They may not say it in those words—in fact, they may not even say the word "cool"—but trust me, it's cool they are looking for.

So go ahead, practice being cool every chance you get. Find your coolest friend and take note of her attitude and how people treat her. Figure out what it is she's doing, and do it. More often than not, you'll find it's what she's *not* doing. She doesn't throw a fit like someone peed in her Wheaties when something doesn't go her way. She doesn't get her knickers in a twist when things change. And she certainly isn't loud and obnoxious when she's out in public. So keep your pickiness in check, be open to trying new things, and go with the flow. The best part? In addition to attracting men, you'll live longer and have more fun because you are undeniably COOL!

5

Four Seasons

nstant attraction is great. It's spectacular. Heck, it's what you want! But it takes time to really get to know someone. I'm a firm believer that it takes four seasons—or one year, if you want to be cut and dry about it—to really get to know a person. It takes time. It takes experiences. It even takes a bit of head-butting sometimes.

Bluelight Special

Sharon meets Jack while walking her dog in the park and they instantly hit it off. They both love animals. They're both from the Midwest. Both die-hard liberals. And they both had a dog named Buddy growing up.

Five months go by with fun evenings out, long walks with the dogs, cooking meals together—just having an overall blast. One Saturday during their sixth month of dating, they're in the car on the way to dinner when blue lights start flashing behind them.

Sharon: Uh-oh. How fast were you going?

Jack: Shit! I can't get pulled over!

Sharon: I know, that sucks. Maybe he'll let you off with a warning.

Jack: No, you don't understand. I *can't* get pulled over. Do you think I can lose him?

Sharon: What?! What's going on?

Jack: Um . . . there might be a warrant out for my arrest.

Sharon: A warrant! What are you talking about?!

Jack: Well, I might have accidentally committed a hit and run last month.

Sharon: WHAT?!?!?

Jack: I'm sorry, I should have told you. It happened so fast. I didn't know what to do.

Sharon: You didn't know what to do? You hit someone in your car and your first instinct was to run?

In an instant, Sharon discovered that her perfect guy was not so perfect. It was hard to validate all those common interests and fun experiences as Jack was being handcuffed on the side of the road. She had to decide if this was a deal-breaker. Sure, Jack was active, outgoing, smart, and funny. On the other hand, he was also irresponsible and unconscionable. If he had no qualms about pulling a hit and run, what else would he be fine with?

Well, she didn't stick around to find out. Sadly, what seemed to be a match made in heaven was only a mirage. The good news? Sharon expertly dodged what could have amounted to a long life filled with deceit and shady morals.

Time Is On Your Side

So many people think that once they find their other half, they must hurry up and seal the deal or else it will disappear faster than Mel Gibson at a Black Panther party. Not true. Dating is a long, thrilling ride, so strap yourself in and get comfortable.

The initial basis for the Four Seasons rule might sound a little extreme, but I've heard enough horror stories that I have to include this. Studies show that it takes about six months to find out if someone has a serious personality disorder. It also takes a good amount of time to figure out if someone is lying about himself. There is no other way to discover these things than through time.

I'm not telling you to log every single word he utters and start to worry if he wavers in the tiniest detail; I'm advising you to listen to your inner voice. If you find that his personal information varies every time you speak to him or he tells you things that you feel just can't be true, put your radar on high alert. If something sounds funny, it's completely acceptable to ask a question to clarify. If he gets defensive with his answer, take it as your first clue that something's up.

Jake's Girlfriend: Hey, Jake? I thought you said you were going to grad school at night. I haven't seen you go to any classes. When do they start?

Jake: Oh, well, that's because I'm taking classes online. I do all my work late at night when I get home and on the weekends in my spare time.

Does this answer work for Jake's detective girlfriend? About 90 percent. Sure, we're in the digital age and tons of people take classes online. She just finds it odd that he never mentioned the online component from the start. Jake's girlfriend would be even smarter if she asked him what classes he's taking. This isn't being nosy; it's being involved with the person you're involved with!

If he's happy to discuss his classes and his goals, he's more than likely telling the truth. If he jumps down her throat and gets defensive, you can bet your lunch money he's lying. I like to think that most people are on the up and up; however, there are some sharks in this sea and it can only help you in the long run if you remain aware.

You know the old saying "If this is the love of a lifetime, you'll have a lifetime to enjoy it"? Live by it. Go slowly and ask questions as appropriate. Take time to experience things together. Enjoy it! If you find out six months into it that Mr. Fantastic is actually Mr. Falsifier, you'll be glad you didn't run to Vegas to tie the knot.

My second reason for the Four Seasons rule is simply that nothing shows how people handle different situations better than time. You can't experience all manner of life events in one month. It's just not possible. You won't know how he handles jealousy until you run into your ex-boyfriend (with whom you are still friends) at a club. You won't know what he thinks about child rearing until your friend with an unruly toddler comes over and you discuss it. You can't know how he handles a sticky situation until you get in a fender bender.

You won't know how he treats his family until you meet them. My mother also told me that you can tell a lot about a man by the way he treats his own mother. Is he kind and sweet to her? Does he offer to help her out? If so, chances are good that he will show you the same kindness and respect. Does he talk down to her and belittle her? If so, run for the hills! Or is he so close to his mother that he worships her in a weird "call Dr. Freud" kind of way? Do you find that he wants you to wear the same perfume as her? Note: This is not the same as baking brownies with her recipe. You may want to double-check that the umbilical cord was actually cut.

Knowing how your man handles tough situations will prove to be very important as you become companions. Think about how his actions will translate to the road bumps in your relationship. The way you handle challenges—and each other—will be a strong indicator of how your relationship will progress in the future.

I would much rather date someone for a year and find out that he's just not the right person for me than rush into a relationship that seems hot, lock it down, and get married in six months—only to divorce two months later. Did I mention that if this is the love of your life, you will have your entire life to enjoy each other?

Hey, Asshole!

Emily loves that each time she experiences something new with her boyfriend, Paul, she gets more insight into him. Recently they were at a crowded outdoor concert and a guy who is completely drunk tries to rush the stage and staggers right into Paul, practically knocking him over. Drunk guy looks at Paul with unfocused eyes and mutters, "Sorry, dude!" Paul takes it all in stride. "That's okay, man, the stage is in front of you. Just keep your eyes open and keep walking straight." Emily was so proud of Paul. He could have easily been annoyed at the situation. He could have seen it as a chance to prove his manhood and gotten all aggro and yelled at the drunk guy to watch where he was going. Instead, Paul took the high road. They were at an outdoor concert. People were having fun. Nobody got hurt. It was just an accident. Paul treated it as such and spun the situation positively. Now this was a guy and that was an attitude that Emily looked forward to seeing for years to come.

Dating may be a game, but it's not a race. This isn't a sprint; it's a marathon.

6

A Little Insight Concerning
the Opposite Sex

The men. The boys. The guys. Whatever you want to call them—they're different from us. Sure, there are the obvious traits and habits—hair, body odor, standing up to pee. There's more than that though. They think differently and act differently—especially when it comes to dating. After many years of trying to understand what goes through their heads, I've finally figured it out. How? I went straight to the source: I asked guys—lots and lots of guys.

Soul Mate Searching

Surprise! After some obligatory hooking up, most men are looking for a soul mate—just like most women. A man wants a true team partnership. He's looking for quality, and he's looking for trust. He can picture in his head what he wants, just like you do, but you won't find him sitting around pining over his fictional blushing bride.

My friend Matt says that girls have a list a mile long about what they're looking for in a man, and a guy can count what's most important to him on one hand. It's not that guys are looking for less; it's just that they are less specific. His dream girl doesn't have to be a certain height with a certain hair color. She doesn't have to love sunsets and love letters, or drive a certain car. Matt says his dream girl has to be cool and smart. And there's got to be a large dose of chemistry. He wants to see her as his friend—and his lover.

Matt's number one complaint? "I hate girls who can't be themselves." He can't stand it when women pretend to enjoy things they don't actually like doing or do the things he does just because he likes them. "I want her to be her," he says.

Matt isn't the only guy who holds steadfast to that belief. The number one complaint that I hear from men is that women pretend to be something they aren't.

A Simple Mind

Men don't overthink dating as much as we do. They don't sit at home analyzing every word of your last conversation. Can you really see two guys sitting around having a conversation like this?

Bob: Hey, Gary? Do you think when Lilly said she would talk to me later that she really meant later like later today or later like tomorrow?

Gary: Well, how did she say it? Was it lighthearted and happy or did it have an ominous tone to it?

Bob: Well, maybe it was ominously lighthearted.

Gary: Oh, in that case dude, forget it.

Seriously, they'll never dissect your texts or seek out something cryptic in your last voicemail. They take things on face value. Why is it that as women we try to complicate things? We're always looking for the trick or the catch.

Playing Dumb Is Dumb

As I look back at the many phases of my life and all the different (wacky, desperate, embarrassing) ways I tried to get boys to talk to me, I realize just how silly the whole quest was.

My first great idea was to play dumb. After all, who hasn't seen men fawn over absolutely beautiful, staggeringly unintelligent women? It's about as dumb as it sounds though. The success rate of attracting guys by playing dumb is right about on par with the success rate of getting a guy by actually being dumb.

I was a sophomore in high school when I first put on the doe eyes, blonde hair, and goofy giggle. I answered questions with a long drawn-out "Whhhhaaaaat?" and a sweet-cheeked "I don't know." I'm embarrassed to say it, but I had a goofy head bob too. Finally a good guy friend approached me and said, "Marina, I know you're not stupid and this playing dumb shit is so unattractive. Please stop it now. No guy likes a dumb girl."

That was all he had to say. I can only hope that playing dumb is a behavior limited to teenagers and that no woman over the age of seventeen is actually trying it to attract guys. It all stems from a lack of self-confidence—we think we're not good enough, so we play dumb. Sounds dumb, right?

You Can't Fake It

Tina heard that running clubs were a great place to meet men. Now, Tina is many things, but a competitive runner she is not. The only time you might catch Tina running would be if someone were chasing her. But she thought, *Hey, a little jogging can't kill me.* So she signs up for a local runners club, and sure enough, on the first group run she meets Ed. Ed was dashingly handsome, super-fit, and charismatic. His first question to her was, "How long have you been into running?"

Tina: I love running! My whole family runs. I was on the cross country team in high school and I run all the time!

Ed: That's awesome. I used to run cross country as well. What did you usually run?

Tina: (Oh shit! She has no idea what to say.) Ha! You are so funny! I can't believe you ran cross country too! Oh my gosh—that was so long ago and I can't remember what I had for lunch yesterday.

Ed laughs and they begin dating. They hit it off and soon discover that they share many of the same interests and goals. The topic of her high school running career doesn't come up again until many months down the road when he takes her to meet his parents.

In talking about their shared interests, Ed brings up the "fact" that Tina ran cross country in high school. By this time, Tina is sweating in her running shorts. She likes this guy. She loves him! She wants to be a part of his life and she feels crappy that she began all of this on a little lie because she thought he would like her if she were more athletic.

Tina finally confesses to her false running career when she and Ed are alone at the end of the night. She tells him the truth—about how she assumed he wouldn't like her if she wasn't an avid runner. Ed accepts her apology and wonders why she would ever do something like that.

Ed: Why do you think I would love you more if you were a runner? Don't you think I wouldn't love you for you?

Tina: I guess not. But I'm glad I told you.

We know that men are out there. We see them all the time. There must be one perfect match for each of us, right? It's true. But only through dating and sharing can you find your true soul mate.

Sure, there will always be the douche bag out there who embarrasses himself by chasing around girls half his age in search of that prizewinning trophy wife. Of course, we have respect for ourselves. We'd never be *that girl.*

We think that if we are someone else—an intellectual, a party girl, a socialite, an athlete—we might attract a certain someone. Truthfully, you don't want to be with anyone you meet under false pretenses. A little lie can quickly grow into a huge web of lies. Pretty soon you'll be forgetting your own name.

I've never met a man who said he wanted his girlfriend to be anything other than herself around him. That goes for whether they're behind closed doors or out in public. Men want someone who is kind, smart, fun, and shares similar interests. They want someone they're physically attracted to. Most of them want a family. They want pretty much the same things we want. By being yourself and having a life that is all your own, you have the ability to meet the person who will truly be your perfect someone.

7

---•

Where to Find Them

What if I told you that you'll probably meet the man of your dreams while you're out doing something that you love to do? Would you beat your clenched fists on the table in a fit of frustration, wondering why you've gone out of your way to be in the right place at the right time among the right group of people, awaiting that magical introduction? Would you say, "Why, for so long, have I gussied myself up to attend silly speed-dating events and corporate mixers, when I should have just been kayaking, wine-tasting, or mud-tugging in the Warrior Dash?"

Opposites Attract—But Not For Long

The truth hurts, and it pains me to tell you this, but yes, you've wasted your time. The fact couldn't be more obvious—and effortless. The best places to find men that you might actually like to meet are the places you actually like to go.

It is of the utmost importance that you find a mate with similar interests. I don't care what anyone says; if you don't share at least some of the same hobbies, it will never work out in the long run. I'm not saying you both have to love Vietnamese food, fried oysters, and tiramisu—or want the same book on your deserted island—but if you both can't find joy in at least some of the same activities, foods, places, and friends, then there's just nothing to work with.

The old saying "opposites attract" is a misnomer in a way. Opposites do attract in relationships because the carefree artsy girl loves the conservative banker because he has qualities she admires. She loves him for his ability to balance a checkbook; he loves her for her ability to fly by the seat of her pants. This is great in the beginning because each person gets exposed to a different lifestyle, which—no doubt about it—can be enlightening. When it comes down to meeting in the middle, however, both parties will decide they much prefer their own rules. Art girl wants to follow her instincts and banker boy needs every move mapped out. They will end up butting heads, and in most cases, their differences will outweigh their respect for each other's personality.

Lobby Your Hobbies

This simple exercise will help you figure out some great places to meet people with similar interests. It will also help you quickly answer that often-asked question "So, what do you like to do?" Get out your pen and paper and make a list of your top ten interests. Any ten things you enjoy doing. From there, list two places you can experience each hobby. Then take each one of those places and evaluate them to see if there's potential to meet someone. For example:

Photography ➜ Photography class or a photography exhibit at a local gallery or museum ➜ Tons of potential!

Okay, I realize that not all hobbies have two places of interest, and not every place has huge potential. Just follow along. Now that we have broken down some of your interests, let's further identify some opportunities to meet people. By meeting people, I mean a fabulous man for you.

For instance, I have a good friend who signed up for a photography class and then went to Italy to shoot with the group. She met her husband on that trip. She's now living in Europe with a beautiful daughter and a wonderful partner in crime! Don't be afraid to check out something that takes you beyond the scope of your own backyard. Attending a local photography exhibit at a gallery is the perfect chance to mingle with fellow enthusiasts. People at the event obviously have an interest, or they wouldn't be there! Strike up a conversation with someone about something you notice and see where it takes you.

Let Chance Do Its Thing

I know, I know. One of the most annoying things a single person can hear from her happily coupled-off friends is "You'll meet him when you least expect it." Oh, and they always say it in that wispy, rosy-cheeked, oh-so-happy tone that makes you want to slap them, don't they? Well, I'm saying it, but only in an effort to encourage you to live your life and be open to all situations. Don't believe me? Here are two real-life stories of success.

Just a Ride to Jackson

It all began on a flight from New Orleans to Houston. Ellen was traveling for work and happened to be sitting around a few guys she knew from her apartment complex when they introduced her to another guy, Alex, a friend of theirs who was also on the flight. After the obligatory "Hi, hello, how's it going," they went their separate ways.

A few days later on the return flight, Ellen was sitting with some of the same guys when one of them remarked to her that Alex would make a really good husband someday. Ellen thought this was the weirdest comment she had ever heard a guy say about a friend of his. Plus, she had met Alex only once and hadn't shown any interest in him, so why should she care if he was husband material? The comment stuck in her head because it was such a strange thing to say.

It just so happened that Alex also lived in Ellen's apartment complex in New Orleans. There was a bar on the first floor of the building where people would often stop by for a drink before going out. Just a week after the "good husband" comment, Ellen ran into Alex there. They chatted about all sorts of things, and then Alex asked Ellen if she'd like to do dinner sometime.

He also told her he was going to Jackson, Mississippi—his hometown—which also happened to be where her mother and stepfather lived. He asked her if she wanted to ride along to visit them. Sure, it seemed a little soon—he was going the next weekend after all—but why not?

It also happened to be his high school reunion weekend. "Since you're coming with me," he said, "how would you like to be my date?" Even though she had to cancel dinner with a good guy friend, she said yes. She just couldn't think of a reason not to go!

Guy Friend: What? You're breaking our date to go with a guy you don't know on a road trip to Jackson?

Ellen: It's not a big deal. It's just a ride to Jackson!

Guy Friend: OK, so I'll see you when you get back?

Ellen: Of course! Like I said, it's no big deal!

Well, Alex and Ellen ended up talking—no awkward silences—the entire three-hour drive. When they got to the reunion, she watched the way he interacted with people and saw what good relationships he had with all of his friends. By the time the weekend was over, she adored him too! Forty-four years later, Ellen's friends still joke with her about that trip—which ended up being so much more than just a ride to Jackson.

The Wedding Date from Diaper Days

My friend Brandon's mom was getting remarried and she asked him to emcee her wedding. At the church, just before the ceremony, a young woman approached Brandon and said hello—with a big beaming smile. When he realized she was an old friend of his named Janice, whom he hadn't seen in at least ten years, a vibrant wave of memories flashed in his mind.

Their mothers had been best friends. Brandon and Janice met when he was two and she was just seventeen days old. They grew up together until Janice was four and her family moved away. Sure, they'd seen each other a few times over the years, but it had been so long. He couldn't believe they were in the same room again!

Needless to say, the alcohol flowed perfectly to all the right party cells, and a fabulous time was had by all. After a night of dancing, a sweaty Brandon went to say goodbye to Janice. "I think she made a conscious decision to keep me that night because she wouldn't let go of my hand," he says.

That night was followed by almost two years of long-distance dating. When she couldn't take being away from him any longer, Janice put her law career on hold to live with Brandon for a year while he finished grad school. They finally landed jobs in the same state, where they now have a two-year-old daughter (and another one on the way), two dogs, and a house.

They love to talk about those early years. They even have a home video that shows them splashing around in a kiddie pool. When Janice gets sprayed in the face with a water hose and starts to cry, Brandon hugs and kisses her until she stops. Brandon likes to say, "You had me at 'Wahhh!'"

8

The Approach

You have to have guts. And you have to use them. I'm a naturally outgoing person, so striking up a conversation with a complete stranger is just second nature to me. However, I realize that to some people, there's nothing more difficult.

Worse Things Could Happen

Here's a good brain game to get you motivated: Think about the worst thing that can happen. If you approach a guy and he rejects you, what's the worst that can happen? Nothing. He wasn't interested. So what? Were you on a stage in front of five thousand people who watched you get the cold shoulder? Do you think your picture will be in the newspaper tomorrow? Do you really think anyone noticed?

Now that you know the worst that can happen—nothing—do the reverse. What's the worst situation that could stem from you *not* approaching him? You'll never know, that's what. I don't know about you, but I don't want to live my life with regrets. *What if? I should have. I wish I had.* Are you scared yet? Good.

Still gun-shy? Practice when it doesn't count. Say hello to someone in line at the grocery store. Ask a random person for the time. Build up to a harmless question: "Where did you get that jacket?" "Do you like your hybrid vehicle?" "I haven't tried the new cherry mocha; is it any good?"

Remember, a smiling person is an approachable person. Smile at someone on a walk. (It really is contagious.) You want to be approachable in case someone wants to ask you a question. Once you're comfortable chatting up total strangers you aren't interested in dating, you'll see how easy it is to approach the ones you are.

It's Just a Question

My friend Linda is painfully shy. As in, she has trouble asking someone to pass the salt at the dinner table. She's so shy that it's a miracle in and of itself that we are even friends. Linda desperately wants to get over her shyness and meet someone, though. She's willing to try to put herself out there a bit, so I volunteer to be her wingwoman—but only if she promises to catch the ball when I throw it and not leave me hanging. She agrees. We devise a plan based on Linda's strongest interest: She's a dog person.

She loves her dog, she loves your dog—heck, she loves anything on four legs that goes *woof.* Really. So we decide to take her Lab Steve (yes her dog's name is Steve) to a new indoor dog park. This is the true story of Linda and her question.

We get to the dog park on a Saturday morning around 10 a.m. There are about twenty people there with their dogs. Our plan is to simply enjoy ourselves, play with Steve, and if we see anyone of interest to Linda, talk to him. We're not going to force it—we're just going to have fun.

After about thirty minutes, we get so caught up chatting about Steve and his problem of sniffing every dog's bum (we nicknamed him Inspector Bum Sniffer), that we decide we should get him a little fedora, a mini notebook, and a pipe for the next time we come to the park. Linda starts pretending to write in a fake notebook about the golden retriever that must smell like bacon because Steve can't stop smelling her. Out of the blue, a nice-looking guy with a black Lab approaches us.

Pete: I've been watching you two for the past five minutes and I just have to know—what is so funny?

(Linda freezes. I jump in.)

Me: Honestly? Linda's dog Steve has a butt-sniffing problem and we were thinking of signing him up for Inspector Sniffer School.

Pete: (Chuckling.) That's funny. (Points to Linda.) So I take it you're Linda? Where's your dog?

Linda: He's the yellow Lab with his nose to that golden retriever's butt.

Pete: Ha! What a great dog! I'm Pete, and this is Remo. (Silence. I look at Linda with a *This is your chance! Say something! Anything!* look. More silence. Then finally . . .)

Linda: Your dog is beautiful. I love Labs. How old is he?

Now, this may not sound like the question of all questions, but it was for Linda. Linda and Pete talked about how old his dog was, how old her dog was, and how many Labs they both have had in their lives. It turns out Pete was new in town and didn't know many people. He asked Linda for her number so they could get the dogs together again. I am happy to say that three years later, Linda and Pete are living together with their two Labs and having the time of their lives.

This all happened because we were doing something we enjoyed, we were having a good time, and Linda opened her mouth to further a conversation when the opportunity presented itself. Sure, the situation could have gone many different ways. Pete could have not had a sense of humor, or he could have had a girlfriend and just wanted to say hi. That's not what happened, though. The situation went the way it went because Linda put herself out there by asking a simple question.

The Hail Mary

Otherwise known as simply going for it. I have a favorite saying: *If you don't ask the question, the answer is always no.* You have nothing to lose except the potential of a great partner. Here's how it works: Once you have located the man you would like to get to know, follow these simple steps. Depending on your situation and location, think of a question you can ask him that's related to where you are and what you're doing.

Don't ask him what kind of toothpaste he uses or what kind of car he drives. Keep it light and keep it relevant to the situation. Poking fun at something around you is a great segue into conversation. You could be a little facetious while waiting in line and remark on the joys of waiting. Or maybe you're at a bar waiting for a friend and you notice a guy waiting as well. More than likely you're both tinkering on your smartphones. You could say, "I need a new app while I'm waiting. What are you currently loving?"

The goal is to have a nice little conversation and hopefully exchange phone numbers. Before you even approach him, you have to remember to be cool and be yourself (remember chapters one and four?).

It's not a quiz and you're not a reporter. You're just a cool gal asking a cool guy a cool question. Less is more. Say hello and ask your question. From there, see if you can keep the conversation going based on his response. If he's friendly and responsive, go ahead and introduce yourself.

The real Hail Mary part comes in here: Let him know how much you've enjoyed talking to him and ask if he wants to talk another time. Ask him if he would like your number. He will either say yes or no. If he says yes—congratulations! You have the potential for a great date. If he says no, be cool. Make a joke. Say, "Ha! I must have talked your ear off already. Have a good one!" Or "Okay, thanks. It was nice talking to you. Have a good day!" Sure it sucks and you may feel rejected, but hey, you only knew him two minutes. Seriously, only two minutes and you put yourself out there! Buy yourself a drink. You've done well.

Tap, Tap

True story: I'm at a concert with my good friend Julie. We're there to enjoy the music and have a good time. I happen to see a very good-looking guy standing next to us. As you know, I'm an outgoing person, and a few cocktails had been consumed, so my confidence was actually intensified.

I lightly tap him on the shoulder, and he turns around with a smile, which is always a good sign. I ask him how he likes the show. Next thing I know we're yapping away about everything under the sun. At the time, I was recently divorced and thought I should get my two big potential deal-breakers out in the open right away. I tell him I'm divorced with two children. (No sense wasting an evening if he isn't going to be cool with that.) I cringe and wait for him to gasp and run away, but instead he starts joking about marriage, divorce, and his family, and we're off on a new tangent. It was instant attraction. We ended up chatting all night, dancing and kissing as if we had known each other for years!

I wasn't necessarily going for the Hail Mary, but I did take a chance. I put myself out there and hoped for the best. My effort, combined with a bit of luck (he could have been uncool or had a girlfriend, after all), and *voilà!* I found my soul mate. Isn't it scary to think I wouldn't have found him if I hadn't tapped him on the shoulder? Sometimes you just have to make the first move. You can't sit on the bench and expect to hit a home run. You have to step up and take a swing. We're still together, crazy in love, perfect for each other. So there.

9

Lookin' for Love Online

have to say I'm not a huge fan of online dating. If you're reading this and you're one of those people with countless horror stories of online encounters, then you share this opinion. However, this is the twenty-first century and the prospect of meeting your man online must absolutely be considered.

Clever Phrases and Carefully Doctored Photos

I'm not going to lie to you. I know a few people who have met someone via an online dating service. I have seen it work out. According to a Match.com study, one out of every five couples these days met online. Impressive stat, yes, but that leaves the majority of us still meeting people face to face.

Why am I not a fan of online dating? It's not that I'm not a fan of opening the doors to meeting new people, it's just the flaws of the World Wide Web that give me pause. Online communication takes away a certain intimacy factor. It's easy to hide behind clever phrases and carefully doctored photos. I prefer to see the whites of a person's eyes the moment I'm introduced to him. There is no better way to detect a rat or a liar than to look into his eyes.

Meeting someone in person is also a great way to see if he actually has friends. Most sociopaths go it alone, and let's be honest, you don't want a psycho. Last, there is something so nice about meeting people the old-fashioned way—in a bar!

If you absolutely must go the online dating route, proceed with caution and try to get a harmless coffee get-together out of the way as soon as possible. This will keep you from wasting your time on someone who is everything but what he says he is.

Not So Random

I am a fan of social networking. For me, it's vastly different than online dating. Facebook is a great way to reconnect with old friends—and meet friends of friends. Please don't fall into the trap of only Facebooking each other though; you've got to get out and meet people in the real world. A social networking site that lets you connect only with people you know can provide you opportunities to revisit old acquaintances. I'm not talking about digging up every ex-boyfriend since the fifth grade to see if they have somehow matured into Brad Pitt. (Although I do have a high school friend who reconnected with his high school sweetheart nineteen years later. They were both divorced and met up for old times' sake. A few months later they got engaged!)

So you never know. But I'm mostly talking about reconnecting with old friends who can introduce you to new ones. As years go by, people move around, expand their interests, and meet more people. Perhaps one of your old friends loves art just like you. Perhaps she has this great single guy friend who's an artist. You can all meet up to talk art. At the very minimum, you get to reconnect with someone from your past.

You can't just go around scoping out your friends' friends for good-looking people and friending them. If you're interested in cruising the open seas, you're better off on eharmony.com. People find it creepy when you ask to be their "friend" and they have no idea who you are. Do you see how online interaction can get a little weird? So again, use this tool to expand your friendship network. Reconnect with people you like. From there, you never know what can happen!

A Prince in Hiding

Amy, a strong-willed thirty-one-year-old who's a successful real estate agent with a penchant for wine and travel, is browsing Match.com one Sunday evening and comes across a potential date. Rob is a six-foot-one marketing manager who lives in the city, likes Indian food, and plays soccer. The picture of him balancing a soccer ball on his head while chugging a beer is a little goofy, yes, but Amy's no buttoned-up straight-edger herself. Besides, his profile is promising. Amy's in a recreational soccer league too and has been known to enjoy a frosty beverage—or four—in postgame celebrations.

After the standard initial greeting—*Hi, I play soccer too. Want to chat sometime?*—Rob comes back with a refreshing response—*Awesome! Your profile looks great. Can I call you tonight?* Not much of a phone-talker, but impressed by his confidence, she gives him her number. That night they talk for two hours in a comfortable exchange that's totally lacking in awkward silences. Turns out Rob's never been to one of Amy's favorite places, the local arboretum. They agree to meet there and have a conversation-filled stroll past the bucolic acreage of pecan trees and tulip beds. It's comfortable, like hanging out with a longtime friend. No pressure. No awkward hand-holding or hugs goodbye.

Date number two is a wine and cheese tasting. Amy likes that Rob prefers urban adventures to obligatory dinner-and-movie outings. Strangely, there's still nothing beyond the fun experiences and pleasing conversation. Date number three: Baseball game. Still no action. Could Inventive Adventure Guy be . . . gay?

Date number four: a picnic dinner replete with cloth napkins and *beurre blanc* sauce all but confirms our Amy's fear. Her pride dies a little with each bite of skewered steak. There is only one thing left to do.

She invites him to her place afterward, casually unraveling her ponytail in one sexy, fell swoop as she snuggles up to him on the couch. "Stay a while," she insists, slowly scooching in his direction with a whole-hearted laugh. Soon she goes in for the kiss. Hooray—he's not gay! In fact, all bodily indicators are pointing in one direction—to his heterosexuality.

It's time to take this research project to the bedroom for final analysis. She goes down to further inspect the goods. Ladies, it's not often that the term "metal mouth" surfaces as the result of attempting oral sex with a stranger, but our poor friend Amy had found herself in quite the stainless steel debacle. Rob was the proud bearer of a Prince Albert piercing, which, if you want to get scientific about it, is an eight-gauge curved barbell that goes in through the frenulum (more informally known as the head) and out the urethra (yes, that's the pee-hole).

Let us not forget that he also had two door knockers on his male breasts—yes, nipple piercings. Had she known, our poor Amy would have knocked before she went downstairs. Had he been a little smarter, he would have warned her of his adornments.

Secrets Are Okay—Sometimes

Do you need to tell your date about every facet of your life? No. In fact, this kind of behavior is strongly discouraged (see chapter two). There are no rules about disclosing piercings, tattoos, scars, stretch marks, or any other bodily adornments—especially early on. Use your judgment, especially if you've been on a few dates and you think things may soon become more intimate. Just a little forewarning can avoid an awkward encounter. Penis piercings aren't necessarily a bad thing, guys, but most girls like a little "heads-up" (pun intended) on any nether-regions jewelry.

10

What to Do When
Nothing Works

Sometimes it may feel as if you have tried everything. You're in shape, you've tweaked your wardrobe, you've been tirelessly frequenting all your favorite places, and talking to total strangers. You've asked all of your friends to set you up. Still, no good guys. What's a girl to do?

A New Outlook

Change your attitude. It's not that nothing works. It's just that nothing has worked *yet*. I know how it is when you want something. You feel like you have to have it yesterday. You've heard the phrase "a watched pot never boils." It's true! Sometimes things don't happen when you want them to. There are two options: Close up shop or refocus. I think you know which way I'd like you to go. So come on, look at your glass as half full!

If you aren't finding what you're looking for, take a step back. It may be because you're looking for the wrong thing! As girls, it's ingrained in our brains that someday we are to find a husband and get married. It's everywhere! Everyone is talking about it, people are doing it, there are commercials for rings, honeymoons, and couples' activities. Why does it seem like you see even more of these things when you're single? Holy power of marketing!

Great Settlers

This great marketing power and peer pressure are to blame for a trap that I think many people fall into. Settling. We date and date and date. Some of these dates are just plain awful, some are boring, and some are just okay. As we get older, we start to question ourselves: Am I being too picky? Am I looking for the impossible? We end up in a two-year relationship with a nice guy by default. The conversation goes like this:

Kristen: How can you not like Mike? He's tall, smart, good looking, super nice, and he adores you! He'd make a great husband and father.

Nicole: Well, I guess you're right. He is great. He is super nice and we get along. All the other guys I've dated are assholes or losers, or they cheat on me. I mean, a good guy like this doesn't come around all the time, right? I guess I should marry him.

What? Seriously? Does anyone see what is wrong with this picture? The hugely important missing piece of this conversation is "I am so in love with him! I can't imagine being without him." "I like it" and "It's nice" are part of the conversation about buying a car you plan to drive for the next five years. That's not how you decide on a husband! This is the great problem in our society. We've lost sight of what a relationship is really about. This fast-paced life we live forces us to quickly get to the next step before we even know what that step really involves.

Husband Hunting— The Truth and the Fairy Tale

As we grow up, the pressure to find a husband gets stronger and stronger. I'm here to tell you, looking for a husband is about as smart as looking for a dog just because you need to go on a walk. Stop the search. Right now.

"Husband" is such a blanket term. By definition it's a man joined to another person in marriage. This sounds to me like a dude with a ring on his left hand who pays the bills and shows up for family photos. Does that sound exciting to you? Think about what it is that you really want with another person. Write down all the things you want to enjoy with that person. Your list may look something like this:

- Someone to laugh with
- Someone to share my thoughts and dreams
- Someone I can cook with
- Someone who loves me for me
- Someone who inspires me to be a better person
- Someone I can't live without

Now that you really know what you're looking for, put your list off to the side. You also know that nobody can make you happy but yourself. What to do? I'm not asking you to put away your dream of sharing your life with someone, I'm asking you to refocus on making a life for yourself. Trust me, in time that life for yourself will include the person you're supposed to be with. You aren't looking for a placeholder in a wedding album—you want something more.

Change of Plans

My friend Nina is thirty-nine. She has been set up with every single man east of the Mississippi. She's been through Match.com, It's Just Lunch, running clubs, book clubs, singles clubs, and practically every bar in the continental US. Until recently she was convinced that there was nobody out there for her. She resolved to start adopting cats and taking needlepoint classes. Then I told her about a famous sculptor who begun sculpting at age fifty. He had never touched this medium before and is now quite famous. He's doing exactly what he loves. He just didn't know he loved it until later in life. Nina thought about that and decided to change the way she lives her life.

Instead of trying and trying and trying to find a man, she decided to find out what Nina wanted to do. She had a great job in advertising but had always wanted to be a teacher. She loved the thought of changing a child's life by being an inspiration and mentor. So she researched different teaching methods and programs and fell in love with the Montessori Method. She found a training center and launched her new career.

Her focus shifted from her usual man-hunting routine to building a life she loved and helping others. Nina spent two years training to become a Montessori teacher and relocated to California upon completion of her training. She was never happier. She had found something she truly loved doing. It was undeniably evident to her students and their parents.

About six months into her first year of teaching, she became close to Laura, the mother of one of her students. They enjoyed talking about the child, the Montessori method, and life. A few months later, Laura asked Nina if she was single. Nina said yes, explaining that she just never found her perfect partner. Laura then tells Nina that her older brother had just moved into town, and she thinks the two of them would really get along. Nina agrees to be set up, and the rest, as they say, is history!

The lesson here is that sometimes we have to reevaluate what it is that we think we want. Sure, Nina wanted to find a man to share her life with. When all she was doing was focusing on that, it just wasn't happening. So she took a step back and decided to make herself happy. In the course of that adventure, she found love.

11

Don't Freak Out

Yay, you! You cleaned yourself up, started smiling, got out there, and landed your dream guy. Hooray! Now don't fuck it up.

Oh, No, You Didn't!

The number one foul a lady can commit is acting crazy. I'm not talking certifiable straitjacket here. I'm talking about runaway emotions that we all seem to have from time to time. Blame it on hormones, blame it on the rain, blame it on the alcohol. Just don't let it go beyond your control.

Sometimes our emotions sneak up on us in relationships. Think about it. Maybe you've never felt so attracted to someone—which can make you feel vulnerable. Maybe you've never had so much fun with someone—which can lead to relationship suffocation. Maybe you've never felt something so real that you're ready to wring the neck of every girl who scopes out your man. Things can be going along swimmingly and then all of a sudden, something happens that you weren't expecting. Wait for it . . . here it comes, the FREAK-OUT! This is when you need to take a step back and check yourself. Before it's too late.

Does That Make You Crazy?

If you have the urge to do any of the following, I hereby dub you Crazy Bitch:

Drive by his house or place of business. This is otherwise known as stalking. If you don't trust him, you shouldn't be with him. Or perhaps the person with the trust issue is you. Seek professional help.

Leave something at his house to mark your territory. Similar to the way a dog would pee on a tree, this is juvenile and tacky.

Accuse every girl who looks in his direction of stealing your man. Men can't be stolen. Dignity can. Keep yours someplace safe.

Rant and rave like a toddler in a toy store when things don't go your way. You're an adult; act like one.

Insert yourself in his life so quickly that you have his mom on speed dial by the second date. Relax and be cool. She will love you in good time.

Leave crazy ranting voicemails or obnoxious e-mails. Now he has proof that you're a crazy bitch.

Whoa, Nellie

So what do you do when something happens that makes you mad or suspicious? First of all, calm down and take a deep breath. Now take another. And another. Do not pick up the phone. I said *do not* pick up the phone. A phone call or text that's fueled by your fear or anger will only lead to chaos. Here are a few steps to get your crazy under control.

Step One: Write down the situation as it happened, truthfully. Not what you imagine in your mind but what actually happened. This means no filling in details when you have no clue, and absolutely no accusations or assumptions.

Step Two: Find a girlfriend who knows you well, knows you can be a bit batty, and loves you anyway. Read her what you wrote down. No fudging!

Step Three: Get her opinion. If it sounds as crazy as yours, call someone else. If it sounds rational, stop freaking out and listen to your friend's advice.

Don't Sweat the Big Stuff—Just Move On

Let's put it all together now. Things happen. Sometimes they're little things, sometimes they're big things. He forgot to call you between his workout and company dinner. Forgivable. Cut him some slack and don't go fantasizing that he's out with some long-legged secretary. Don't even mention it. Just be cool. Hear that? Be cool. Chill out. Relax. Bonus: if he even realizes he forgot to call, he'll be thrilled you didn't bust his balls about it.

Try this one on: It's the fifth time he's "forgotten" to call you, canceled a date, or come home at 3 a.m. with no reasonable excuse. Now it's time to evaluate whether or not this is working for you. His actions don't sound very respectful to me, but there's no reason to go crazy. Simply let him know you expect more from your housekeeper and your friends—and especially your boyfriend. Unless he can give you the respect you deserve, *sayonara* is in order.

OK, so what if you come home and he's sleeping with your best friend in your bed? Sounds like a good time to boil the rabbit, but let's take a step back here. You can't do something like that. Why? Because it's crazy!

Sure, you're hurt. You're insulted and you're embarrassed. You're also very lucky to have found out early in the game that this guy is an asshole and so is your so-called friend. Ask them to leave some cash on the table so you can have your house properly sanitized and politely mention that as you only talk to decent people they need to delete your phone number and e-mail address from their contact lists.

Then, my friend, in private, feel free to say all the crazy-ass shit you've been holding back. Call your *real* best friend and tell her what a rotten dirtbag he and your former bestie are. Then bury it and move on. You don't need crazy and you don't need drama. If you want either of those things, you can watch *Jersey Shore* or *Real Housewives.*

12

Don't Snoop

The number two foul you can commit is snooping. Don't do it. Why? Because snooping is wrong. It's juvenile, and it shows distrust. If you don't trust him, don't date him.

Trust Your Company

More than likely this trust issue is your problem. Did you ever take a step back, look at your past relationships, and figure out that you can't seem to trust anyone? Just one bad experience with a cheating boyfriend and you think it's destined to happen again? I'm here to tell you this is simply not true.

Issues of trust need to be fixed before you can have a healthy relationship. Think back and really figure out where these feelings are coming from. Be rational. Yes, it happened. Just because something happens once with one person doesn't mean it will rinse and repeat.

Don't Be Led By Temptation

I know it's tempting. You notice an e-mail on his desktop just begging to be read. A phone left alone with texts that beckon. The stack of receipts on his nightstand. The list could go on and on. Remember, this is his personal, private information. Truth be told, I'm sure he'd share all of this with you if you asked because he has nothing to hide. Just like you have nothing to hide. Right? So think of it this way: Do you want him sniffing around in your purse? Perusing your e-mail? Eyeballing your phone? Of course not. So don't do it to him.

Sweet Shady Jenny

My friend Bridget swears she was just emptying the pockets of Clint's jeans to do the laundry when the piece of paper "fell out." It was folded up. She was just going to leave the note as is and give it to him, but she just couldn't help opening it up. She almost threw up when she saw what it said.:

Call me! —Jenny! (With a phone number scribbled under her name.)

What? Who the hell is Jenny and why is her number in his pocket? That dirty rotten little shit. Bridget's fists clench, her mind races, and she is officially pissed. She can't decide whether she wants to call Jenny first and find out what the hell is going on or just tape the note to a bag with all Clint's clothes in it as she bids him farewell! My suggestion? Tell him what happened and ask him what's going on.

So Bridget tells him the truth. She was washing his jeans and found the note in his pocket. She felt bad that she looked, and she was sad at what she found. Clint immediately recognizes the look on her face and says, "Oh my gosh! I know how this must look, but honestly, when I was working that conference yesterday (he is a production manager that puts together big conferences) a guy from the company gives me this piece of paper and says, 'That girl over there wanted me to give you this.' I told him that was very sweet, but I had a serious girlfriend. I just put it in my pocket because there was not a trash can nearby. I meant to throw it away and truly forgot."

Logically this makes sense. Bridget and Clint have been dating for more than a year and she has no reason to believe he's up to anything shady. He's a great-looking guy and she can totally see women sending their numbers across the room to him. I mean, you can't blame a girl for trying. You can applaud the guy for being honest. Nothing ever came of it because Clint was telling the truth and Bridget trusted him.

Room for Questioning

If you have reason to believe that something shady is going on, you need to ask him directly. I'm going to warn you, though, if you start quizzing him about every little thing as if you're some kind of detective, he's going to feel interrogated, and he's going to bail. I would too. Constant questioning equals lack of trust. Who wants to be followed around and quizzed about their every move?

So relax and mind your own business or pick up a hobby if the urge to snoop is that strong. I repeat—you cannot have a real relationship if you do not trust someone.

13

Don't Get Ahead of Yourself

S trike three occurs when you reek of desperation and come off as too eager. This gets tricky because your first instinct is to be happy and excited about a new relationship; however, you don't want to appear as if you haven't had a meal in weeks and suddenly a big juicy steak materialized in front of your face. Don't drop all of your plans because a fabulous man asks you out. Work him into your schedule. Never rearrange your life to accommodate a man.

Home for the Holidays

It's mid-October and Sue is having a blast on her third date with Brandon. She can't believe she's finally found such a great guy. She thinks he might even be *the one!*

Sue's family lives out of town, and, being the planner that she is, she's already making her Thanksgiving plans. She really wants to introduce Brandon to her family, and she's already wondering what to get him for Christmas.

Is there anything wrong with Sue being so excited? No. Is there anything wrong with Sue planning for Thanksgiving? No. It's next month, after all. Is there anything wrong with Sue wanting to introduce Brandon to her family on Thanksgiving? Maybe.

This is where things can get hairy. You've had a few dates. You get along great. There's no reason to think you shouldn't plow forward and bring the gang all together, right? Wrong.

It's only date number three. Thanksgiving with the family is kind of a big deal. I'm not saying there has never been a woman in this world who has invited a guy home for the holidays soon after the first date and had things go well. I'm just saying s-l-o-w your roll a bit. Family events are a big deal. They should be reserved for people who plan to be in your life for a while.

Chances are good that if on date number four Sue asks Brandon to meet her family on Thanksgiving or asks him what he wants for Christmas, he might just wig out. I really wouldn't blame him. There is no need to merge all aspects of your lives after a few dates. As time goes on, feelings grow stronger, and he expresses an interest in meeting your family, then by all means, make it happen.

Don't you think you want to have a few months under your belt before you bring a guy to the big family event?

Don't you want to know someone pretty well before Uncle Harry tells everyone about the time you stuffed your mouth with mashed potatoes, then popped your cheeks and proclaimed you were a zit, the way Bluto did in *Animal House?*

Horse. Then Cart.

It's exciting when things start moving along. You begin making plans for the future. You've got tickets to a concert next month or maybe he asks you to come with him to his company's holiday party. He calls you his girlfriend in public. Sometimes we just get excited after three fabulous dates. Things are going well. This is one of the most thrilling moments of a relationship. But it doesn't mean you need to start picking out names for your children.

In terms of relationships, men are in slow motion. Women are sprinters. We have a tendency to plan our lives—you know it's true. That house with the wraparound porch? The private island honeymoon? Some say it stems from childhood fantasies of fairy princesses and horseback rides into the sunset with our knights in shining armor.

I bet you've heard most of your girlfriends start a sentence with "When I get married, I'm gonna . . ." I'll also bet you big bucks that some of them have the location, dress, and flowers all picked out. If you were to ask a single man on the street what his wedding plans were, he'd probably be able to tell you only that they involve a woman.

My advice for you is to stay excited and not lose your zest for romance. Keep your excitement to the present though, or in five years you'll look back at your staid life and wish you'd reveled a little more in those delightful just-started-dating months instead of planning your next steps.

14

Stop, Listen, and Don't Overanalyze

M y friend Betsey gets set up on a blind date. It goes very well. So well, in fact, that she and the guy begin to talk about all the fun things they'd like to do together in the future. The next morning he texts her to say he had a great time and can't wait until the next date. Everything sounds just dandy, right? So why is this the point when most women start dissecting?

Betsey: So, when he says he had a great time, do you really think he means he had a great time?

Me: That's what he said, so I'm going to say yes.

Betsey: When he says he's looking forward to the next date, do you really think he'll ask me out again? Do you think he really likes me?

Me: Betsey, we can only go with the facts. If he says he's looking forward to the next date, then he's looking forward to it. Do I think he'll ask you out again? Yes, it sounds like he will. I have to assume he likes you if he says he had a great time and wants to ask you out again. Unless of course he never calls you again; then he's a liar.

Betsey: So you think he won't call?

Me: Do I look psychic?

Betsey: No. Well, maybe.

Me: Betsey, the facts. He said he had a great time and couldn't wait for the next date. Plain and simple. Now let's just walk away with that. Let's find a hobby or get some work done until the next date.

Betsey: OK, but are you sure?

Me: Stop overanalyzing!

Dissection—Don't Do It

Do you see how the above conversation was completely pointless? We had two sentences in writing that should have been taken as fact. Why do we try to turn things into something they're not or look for some secret meaning? Why does it feel compulsory to dissect every word a man says?

I won't lie to you and say that I haven't derived hours of joy over the years analyzing many a sentence from many a man. It's almost fun. A girlish pastime. I won't lie to you and tell you it isn't asking for trouble either. Overanalyzing is a sign that you need more things to do in your life. If you've got time to sit around for hours wondering if he meant what he said, then it's time to find yourself a hobby.

Here's my advice: Anytime you feel the need to break down a statement from a man you're in a relationship with—stop! Take it on face value and move on to another project that improves your life or someone else's.

I Ain't Trying to Hear That

Consider this act one of the worst relationship offenders. It happens when you have all the evidence in front of you, and rather than see it for what it is, you block it out or remix it to something else. It goes like this: He says one thing and you hear another. Or you hear what he says, and you just don't listen.

When a friend of mine began dating her boyfriend, his divorce had just been finalized. He told her from the beginning that he had no intentions of marrying again, nor did he ever plan to have more children. *He's just saying that because he's recently divorced,* she thought. *In time, he'll see that it's possible to have a successful marriage.*

Flash forward three years to their breakup. She's mad because he refuses to settle down. She wants children. He doesn't. Hold up. Did I miss something? Stop man-bashing already! It's not his fault. He was honest with her from the start, and she didn't listen. The fault lies with my friend who heard what he said but didn't listen to a word of it.

This happens way too often and it makes me totally nuts. Sometimes we want something so badly that we hope in our hearts things will be different if we just turn a deaf ear to all the signs. It's heartbreaking really.

Magic Words

Listen closely. If you hear any of the following phrases or anything similar, take them as the truth and act accordingly. Guys rarely lie with these kinds of statements. Don't take it personally. Don't hold onto the hope that you might change his mind. You won't.

- I don't want anything serious right now.
- I never want to get married.
- I don't want children.
- I can't be monogamous.
- I'm not good with commitment.
- I hate being tied down.

The Truth Shall Set You Free

I'm a creative and optimistic person by nature. I'm a logical person by choice. Logic keeps you sane. I'm not trying to rain on the parades of all the women who have defied the odds by marrying the guy who said he'd never settle down or having children with a man who swore he'd never have kids. Good for you, girls. I hope you are happy. Right now I'm trying to be logical and give advice that rings true *most* of the time. Listen to what he tells you. Look at what his actions say to you. I know you know in your heart what message he's trying to send. If he says he loves you and all actions point in that direction, then bask in that love and return it if you feel the same way. If he tells you he can't be serious right now and his actions back it up, and you aren't happy with that, back out of that relationship and move toward something that makes you happy. We can only look at the evidence that lies in front of us. See the situation for what it is and act accordingly.

15

The Good Times— Sex and Marriage

Sex

Just do it. I am a firm believer in the saying "Try before you buy." Sometimes that piece of fruit looks great on the outside, but once you cut it open, there's no flavor.

Yes, sex is a very personal thing, but it's also vitally important in a relationship. Great sex keeps a relationship on fire. If you don't have chemistry in the bedroom, you can forget about the rest of the rooms. A healthy sex life brings people closer together. It also makes you live longer. So why not? Before you indulge though, understand this: great sex does not guarantee a great relationship.

Sex Doesn't Make You a Slut

Stereotypes exist about women and sex, and I want to dispel a few things. Only you can make yourself feel a certain way. Nobody else can. So if sleeping with someone on the first date doesn't bother you and having multiple partners in the course of your life doesn't bother you, then it doesn't matter. If sleeping with someone before dating for six months makes you feel like a two-dollar hooker, then by all means, wait for that six-month mark. You just have to be honest with yourself.

Everyone has their own beliefs, and they should stick to them (and keep their noses out of other people's business). As long as you're being safe and honest with your mate, relax and enjoy! I'm not talking about working the corner—I'm talking about enjoying sex with your partner!

Behold, the 5 W's of sex and dating:

Who?

The man you want to sleep with, that's who! Physical attraction and chemistry must be in place for a relationship to work. Without the chemistry, the relationship won't last. You'll know if there's chemistry, and you shouldn't have to waste much time figuring it out. If it's there, you'll feel it within the first two dates. You don't have to have sex with someone to feel it; if the chemistry's there, you'll experience it just by standing next to him. If it's missing, find another Who.

What?
Sex, that's what! Nothing like great sex to start (or end) the day!

Where?
Anywhere you like. (Just be careful in public places.) Mix it up, make it fun. Create sexy little secrets you both can share forever. *Remember the time we had sex in the hammock in Hawaii?* Wink wink.

When?
It's up to you. "When" is whenever you feel comfortable. I'm a firm believer in no sex on the first date; however, I know a handful of people who do hit the sack early on, and all is well. My view is that if the relationship is going to work out, you'll have plenty of time to have sex. So I wait. If you're just looking for a little fun and not interested in keeping this guy around, then go for it! On the other hand, if you really like the guy and want to get to know him better, take the time to date before jumping into bed together. How long? It's up to you two. My advice? Take your time.

Why?
Because it feels great, that's why! Sex is a proven stress reliever and mood enhancer. It's great exercise and it releases good hormones in your body. Studies have shown that an active sex life can lengthen your life. Plus, it will bring you closer together.

The M-Word

You guessed it—marriage. By definition it's the state of being united to another person in a consensual and contractual relationship recognized by law. It's what we've been told we need to do since birth, right?

Is that what you really want? A legal contract? Or do you want to find the love of your life? Aren't you looking for someone who completes you? Makes you a better person?

I say take marriage out of the picture. That doesn't meant throw it away. It means get the idea that marriage is the final prize out of your mind. So often dating gets overshadowed by the desire to be married. Where's the fun in that? Don't let dating become a chore that leads to a husband, rather than a quest to find a soul mate.

This is why so many marriages fail. We have a picture in our minds of this husband. He's good looking, he has a job, we have 2.5 kids and a house and an SUV. Everything is perfect. Right? Well, it's right if placeholders and material things make you happy. Ask anyone who knows anything about anything and they'll tell you that you cannot buy happiness. Your SUV and house can't love you back. Just because the puzzle seems to have all the pieces doesn't mean it's finished. If you look really closely at that puzzle, you will find that you can't see the love and joy because you didn't allow room for them.

People see dating as a means to an end. Only after they enter into marriage (because marriage is what they thought they were after) do they find out it's not all it's cracked up to be. So I advise you to forget about marriage for now. Train yourself to think differently. Instead of looking for a husband, look for a good, honest relationship that's based on love, common interests, and respect for each other. This is a beautiful thing. Much more romantic and fulfilling than a legal contract, don't you think?

If you've been dating for a while and you do decide to seal the deal, then do it. Just make sure you do it for the right reasons.

16

Throwing in the Towel

The good—and bad—thing about dating is dating it-self. It's not as easy as knowing that you hate the cold and skiing is not your game. It's more like knowing you like sports but you may have to play a lot of them to find the one you love.

Relationships are the same way. There are so many phases, so many give-it-a-try's. Not only do you have to be attracted to a person, you have to have things in common. We make our way through countless dates and rites of passage before entering coupledom. It may be sooner or it may be later, but sometimes we notice that something isn't quite right. When this happens, it's time to take a closer look.

Three Strikes

Think about it like baseball. Three strikes and you're out. The first strike is harmless—probably just a fly ball. Lucky for you, you caught it in time.

Maybe you figure out that his jokes are a little stale and you find yourself cringing every time he tries out a new one in public. Deal-breaker? Perhaps. Or maybe his positive qualities outweigh his sorry sense of humor. Can you live with it? Would he be receptive if you said, "Hey, dude, I love that you like to joke, but you need some new material. Can I help ya out?"

You'll figure out what's important to you in regard to this person. We all have quirks. They make us who we are. Don't you just want someone to love you for you—quirks and all? Then you've got to be able to tolerate some less than desirable personality traits.

Strike two is close to an out, but it's not. Yet. You can live with his jokes, but now you realize that he takes life a bit less seriously than you'd like him to. Now it's time to really think about what will make you happy in the long run. Is he so go-with-the-flow that he doesn't realize he has to man his own ship? Or is he pleasantly optimistic that things will work out, and while he realizes life has some bumps, he prefers to see them as adventures and not obstacles?

Could it be that you're so one-tracked that it's your way or the highway? Can you agree to lighten up a little? This kind of fundamental difference can easily turn into a deal-breaker, but it doesn't have to. It requires a serious discussion about your goals and the visions you have of your life together. Hammer it out now before the consequences of your actions affect more than yourself.

Strike three is an out. He constantly treats you like crap. You're last on his list of priorities. Everyone is telling you what an asshole he is. Trust me, girls, if your friends say he sucks, more than likely they're right. Your friends know you and love you. They want you to be happy. You are in their best interests. So if everyone who loves you thinks this guy is bad for you—he probably is. Listen to those who love you.

It's Not Me; It's You

Maybe you're in a situation that's not so obvious to the rest of the world. You have a seemingly great guy who's quite the jokester—except the jokes are mostly on you. The first time it happened you thought he was playing around. Then came the second time and the third time. There's still something there that keeps you around though. You've got to look beyond whatever that something is.

Verbal abuse is no laughing matter, but it sneaks into countless relationships only to be tolerated by way too many women. Why? Do we need a companion so much that we will take one at any cost? Is he nice and then not nice and then nice again? The way it happens is different for everyone, but you need to get away. Throw in the towel.

I was unlucky enough to find myself in a verbally abusive relationship pretty early on in my dating career. I was twenty-five years old, confident, and outgoing. I met a man who seemed the same. He swept me off my feet. He was charming and attentive. I thought I had everything I wanted.

Slowly but surely he began to talk down to me. Just a little bit at a time. I barely noticed—but I noticed. The first time I said something about it, he blew me off. Said I was being sensitive. Talked his way out of it. It kept happening and I kept protesting, but he would flip the script and make it sound like I was playing the victim.

I began to doubt myself, but I always knew in my heart that I wasn't the problem. I was alone in my car one day and heard a song that gave me the confidence to know that I wasn't going to sacrifice my self-esteem and self-worth for a man who didn't respect me. If you're being verbally or physically abused, seek help right away. It's not right and you don't deserve it.

A bad relationship is not always going to involve something as serious as abuse, but I'd be doing a disservice if I didn't mention it. Always trust your gut. If something doesn't feel right and you aren't comfortable, talk about it. The first time he says something that offends you, say something. More than likely, he won't even realize he did it and apologize. If he tries to blame it on you or further insult you, get out. This tiger does not change his stripes and his bite only gets worse with time. Remember, it's not you—it's him.

It's tough out there. You have to play a lot of games before you finally win. Sometimes you have to throw in the towel or take a break. It's okay. The biggest mistake you can make is to settle for something that isn't right for you. Life is too short to be unhappy. You're better off being happy with yourself than unhappy with someone else.

You Still Rock

I hope I've steered you in the right direction. I hope you've learned that you can never go wrong by investing in yourself. Be the best person you can be. Enjoy your life. Meet people and be a participant rather than a spectator.

My wish is for you to live your life to the fullest and make it something you can really enjoy. I'm willing to bet that when you're out there living, you'll stumble on that guy you've been looking for.

Appendix

Essential Tips and Answers to All Your Unanswered Questions

—Early On—

Approaching Men
- Be simple and be real.
- Be creative.
- Be yourself, always.
- Look your best.
- Think positive.
- Wear a smile.

Q. There is a guy I really like at work. How should I approach him?

Let's refer to the old saying "Don't shit where you eat." If you decide you want to go for it, just be sure you're ready to quit your job if it doesn't work out. Still certain? Meet for coffee and talk about life. Develop a friendship. If that friendship goes to the next level, go for it, but be aware of the consequences.

Q. I always see the same really cute guy at Starbucks. Is it cheesy to talk to him?

I am a fan of random introductions in public places. First, take note of what he's doing. You need a conversation starter. Ask him a question about said thing. If he responds warmly, engage him a bit further. If it's still going well and he hasn't asked you for your number yet, say you have to run and ask him if he'd like to meet for coffee another time. Remember, if you don't ask, the answer is always no!

Q. I'm afraid to approach men, but nobody ever approaches me. What should I do?

Well, girl, you're going to have to work on your self-confidence. Practice saying hello to strangers—the ones you're *not* attracted to. Work up to giving a compliment to a man you find attractive. Picture yourself being confident. You have nothing to lose by being friendly and starting a conversation. Remember, if you don't ask the question, the answer is always no.

Q. What if I ask a guy out and he tells me he has a girlfriend?

Simple. Say "Oh well, lucky her!" And walk away with a smile.

Texting

- Never use text messaging as a primary form of communication.
- Don't be an obsessive texter. He doesn't need to know your every move—especially via text.
- If you're pissed off, don't send a text.
- Do not try to dissect texts—remember, emotions get lost in transit.
- Beware of sexting.

Q. He texts me all the time, but he never calls. How can I get him on the phone?

Simply call him and say, "Hey, while it's really fun to text, I'd prefer you call me to ask me out." He'll either get it or he won't.

Q. Can I send him a flirty text?

Have you been dating for some time? If so, sure. Just watch the X-rated texts—while sexting is fun with a trusted partner, swapping risqué messages with a new beau is risky. Be wise, young texter.

Q. He canceled a date via text. What should I say?

Nothing. A move that dumb deserves silence. If something truly came up, a real man would have called to tell you.

Q. He keeps texting someone else during our date. What should I do?

Say, "My, you look awfully busy. Perhaps this is a bad time." Anyone who can't give you his full attention doesn't deserve you.

Q. He sent me a text and I can't tell exactly what it means. Should I guess?

Emotions are lost in text messages. Don't jump to conclusions. Ask and confirm instead.

Q. I sent him a text an hour ago and still haven't heard from him. I know he carries his phone with him all the time. Should I be freaking out?

Simmer down, girl. He probably has a life—something you should look into getting.

Q. I sent him a long detailed text and got a very short reply. Do you think he's giving me a hint?

That was your first mistake. If you have something important to say, say it in person or at least on the phone. Guys normally don't text novels. Take it at face value and have a real conversation next time.

Q. I received a text that looked like it was meant for someone else. What should I do?

Let him know you don't understand his last text. He'll look at it and explain.

Q. He left his phone out and I really want to look at his texts. Should I?

No. You must absolutely resist the urge. No snooping! If you don't trust him, you shouldn't be with him. Would you want him looking through your inbox?

Q. I feel like texting is starting to replace real conversations. Texts are cute and all, but I want a real live boyfriend.

I applaud your maturity level. Yes, texting is a nice way to let someone know you're thinking about them, but it's not a replacement for real-life conversations. Tell your shy guy that while you like the attention via text, you'd prefer some face time.

The First Date

- Be cool.
- Relax, he's nervous too.
- Look great but still look like you.
- You're not a hooker—leave something to the imagination.
- Have fun—it's just a date.

Q. What should I wear?

Something that makes you look beautiful and something appropriate for the place, time, and activity.

Q. Who pays?

The person who asked for the date.

Q. What should we talk about?

Whatever comes naturally—your hobbies, your jobs, current events. Remember to keep some things to yourself; now is not the time to tell him about that time you tried acid in high school.

Q. Should he pick me up?

Whatever makes you comfortable. However, it's nice to have your own wheels in case you need to bail.

Q. He invites me over after our first date. Should I go? Should I spend the night?

No and no. If this thing is going to work out, you'll have plenty of time for nookie. I'm not saying you have to wait a certain amount of time, but come on, girls, leave a little to the imagination.

Q. The date is awful. I want to go home, but we're still in the middle of dinner. What should I do?

As much fun as it would be to run right out the door, you are a decent human being. So politely finish dinner, say thank you, and then get the hell out of there.

Q. He's late.

How late? Ten minutes? If he apologizes, let it go. If it's more than twenty minutes and he hasn't called with an explanation, then it's time to call your friends and make other plans. You don't have time for this.

Q. He said he'd call, but he never did. Should I call or text him?

No and no. He's a liar if he said he'd call and didn't. You don't need that.

Q. We're having a great time, but he's putting on some moves that are a little fast for me. I don't want to scare him off, but I don't want to get this close yet either.

Tell him you are having a wonderful time but you'd like to take it a little slower. A good guy will appreciate your honesty and act accordingly. If he doesn't, fire him.

—So You've Been on a Few Dates—

- Catch Your Breath
- Passion and lust are not love at this point.
- Create some space—you don't have to spend every second together.
- Enjoy the newness!
- Find creative, fun things to do together.

Q. We went out on a date last Friday. It's Thursday of the next week and I haven't heard from him. What should I do?

Nothing. If he likes you, he'll call you.

Q. We've been on four dates. Should we have the boyfriend/girlfriend talk?

Only if it feels right. There's no minimum or maximum number of dates required to cross this threshold, but don't rush it. Have the talk when it feels right.

Q. He called to ask if I want to go out—tonight. Do I say yes?

Politely reply, "I'd love to go out with you, but I've already got plans. How about this weekend?" I'm all about spontaneity but only after a decent relationship has been established. At this point, he needs to know you've got a very busy life of your own.

Q. He's making plans for the future that I'm not ready for. How can I slow him down?

Simply let him know how you feel. Honesty is the only card to play.

Q. He's starting to act possessive and wants to know where I am all the time. How do I handle this?

My first instinct is to say run for the hills! But maybe he's just trying to shower you with attention. Let him know exactly how you feel about it. If he does it even one more time, *sayonara.*

Q. He's already talking marriage and kids. It's a little soon. Do I say something?

It's good to know from the beginning that you have the same goals in mind. Someone who doesn't want children would definitely not work for someone who does. However, stick to the Four Seasons rule (see chapter five) before committing to anything this serious.

Q. I think he's dating someone else. What do I do?

Have you talked about it? If you want to be exclusive, you have to tell him. If he says he's not ready, well, he's not ready. Find someone who is.

Q. I'm dating a few people at once. Do I have to tell them?

If you're having sex, you absolutely need to inform all parties involved. If it's just a few dates and you're trying to figure out what's going on, you don't need to disclose. If one of the guys asks, however, you have to be honest. Tell him you're seeing other people until you figure it out.

Sex

- No chemistry? Don't bother.
- There's nothing wrong with "try before you buy."
- Great sex keeps things exciting, but it doesn't guarantee a perfect relationship.
- Stick to your beliefs.
- Don't do anything that makes you feel uncomfortable.
- Be adventurous, but be safe.

Q. When should I have sex with someone?

This is a personal question each of us must answer for ourselves. While I never recommend having sex on the first date (or even the third date), there's no magic number. Do it for yourself and for him, not because you're pressured.

Q. Should I disclose how many sexual partners I've had?

As a rule, I say no. It doesn't matter if you have been with three people or thirty-three—it's always going to be more than your partner wants to hear. As long as you're healthy and disease-free, keep it to yourself.

—Breakups—

- It happens. Get over it.
- If it's not working, don't force it. Cut your losses.
- Be kind. He has feelings, too.
- There is always someone else. Always.

Q. What's the best way to break it off with someone I've only had a few dates with?

The next time he calls to ask you out, simply let him know that while he's a nice guy, you just don't think it's going to work out. Always be nice. Remember, everyone has feelings. You don't have to go on ad nauseam when you've only been on a few dates.

Q. What's the best way to break up with someone I've been dating for a few months?

This deserves a face-to-face meeting. Be kind and let him know gently what the problems are. Hopefully he's mature enough to find your honesty helpful for future relationships.

Q. He broke up with me after only a few dates. Can I ask him what went wrong?

No. As much as you'd love to know what the problem was, you'll probably never get an honest answer. Sometimes the timing is just wrong. Other times it might be something he's too embarrassed to say. Either way, keep your chin up and be cool.

Q. My friends don't like him, but I think they are just jealous. Really? Do your friends like you and care about you? Ask them why they don't like him and truly listen. Chances are they have your best interests in mind.

Q. It's not really working out, but it's not the worst and I hate being single. Should I keep dating him until someone else comes along?

How about NO? Would you want someone to string you along until something better comes along? That's just not nice. Have some self-respect and work on yourself and don't just hang around for free dinners. Certainly you can entertain yourself or find some friends for weekend fun.

About the Author

Marina Sbrochi holds a bachelor of arts in English literature from The Ohio State University. After college, she moved to New York City to hone her dating skills and observations. In her not-so-recent past, she appeared as an actress in a handful of movies, TV shows, and commercials, and was also a sketch comedian and writer for the Dallas-based improvisational comedy group Mass Hysteria. Marina lives in Dallas with her two children and the love of her life.

For more information about Marina, please visit www.StopLookingForAHusband.com.